DICK CHENEY'S HEART

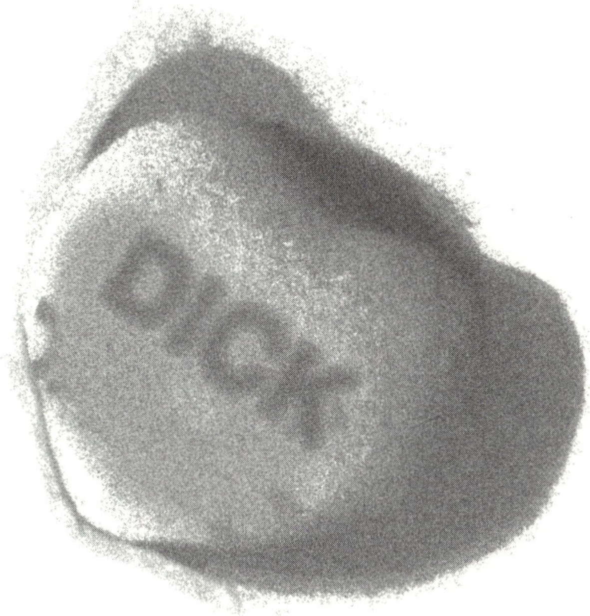

DICK CHENEY'S HEART

HEATHER FULLER

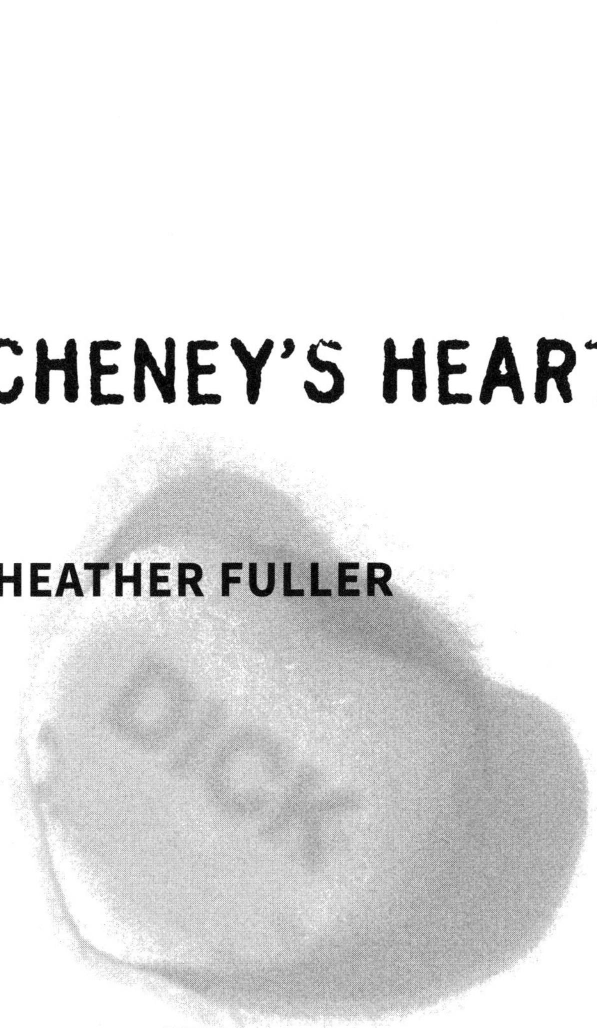

EDGE

ALSO BY THE AUTHOR

perhaps this is a rescue fantasy (Edge Books, 1997)
Dovecote (Edge Books, 2002)
Startle Response (O Books, 2005)

δ

The author extends heartfelt thanks to the editors of the following publications where poems from this collection previously appeared: *Altered Scale, Free State Review, i.e. reader, The Pink Line Project, Tolling Elves,* and *Tripwire.* Thank you also to Michael Ball, Stephanie Barber, Buck Downs, Dan Gutstein, Adam Robinson, Rod Smith, the late and legendary Chris Toll, and Rupert Wondolowski for providing venues for public readings of this material. Further gratitude is in order to Dan Gutstein for first review of "A Memoir."

IN MEMORIAM

δ

David Franks
Chris "Dedalus" Myers
Tom Roder
Leslie Scalapino

Cover photography/composition by Jesse Hill and Audrey Hunter.
Design and typesetting by Deirdre Kovac.

ISBN: 978-1-890311-41-4

Edge Books are published by Rod Smith, editor of *Aerial* magazine, and distributed by Small Press Distribution, Berkeley, CA; 1-800-869-7553; www.spdbooks.org.

Edge Books
P.O. Box 25642, Georgetown Station
Washington, D.C. 20027

aerialedge@gmail.com www.aerialedge.com

CONTENTS

Hand Craft

no chance of a head-on
if you don't ride the road

here from the blue dog hawk wolverine
oratory comes in buttons and closures

hands were installing shoelaces disembodied
but never naming
whalebone corset

in the fabric retrofitting
comfort congregation
hook and eye
canoodle voucher

cards started punching before hands
broke the lie chain
whore train
doves loosed in a quandary

δ

can you remanufacture warshot years
bring back the sense of body

fellating buzzcock soldiers on
and who's piping up

it's just you again carrying on

dying in

reloading
reloading

δ

take a cue from convenience food mouthfeel

you can have your solar power
but people cost 10 cents

experiment of how far run out of town

by the sock monkey bureau
sewn up at the eyes
stuffed in the mouth

measured by the wisdom
to impeach
ripping out seams

out of the way

she's out there again
shaping reality

δ

your remission is this
you will never be in the clear

the diseased body wears its clothes like bindings

vectors cross into the urban
how did we miss this planning pocket

cinched by security
neighbors rose for the searchlight
slept in foxfire

they could not imagine the horror
so they made it real

your country is your phantom limb
all that's left to glean

the cat has no qualms

δ

2003
2004
2005 … knelling

what hands are left to do
while a country betrays them

she kept worrying til she wore clean through

cartilage bathed in broken bottle disembodied

bite off their heads and weeds grow horizontal

δ

stitch dropped in a jury
years at the flywheel

no body wears the coordinates for
the dressing down
outfitting to occupy
bunkers or parlors

darners haystacked underfoot

U.S. Wraps Barbed Wire Around Free Iraqi Village

if poetry the eyes and ears of a wise society
a woman folds into position

will not be fed
from the squander messkit

a woman folds

the cumulus disgust
will not be fed

Data Recovery Project: ***Rascaline***

vigilant in the street for broken things
a bitch can have her eye out
dog-bitch in and out of foundering
on alert for what the hand might do
cut you in your sleep bony
old numbchuck nostalgia

she picked it up
was obliged to keep it
puppyhead in the jaw
where a hangman's knot would snap
what you left on the roadside
underwear splint and ya'll

δ

we must have wanted the whole package
when Jeb is presidente
this oligarch and me we are not on good terms
went down on the docket like WhiteHouse[dot]xxx
but went into the papers as *lately married*

here is where the cat bites the writing hand
the dog demurs in the prospect of begging
the cat wasting for all these mindings countless
warnings eluding human courtesy tune in
to ears tails hackles
in the bandit aggregate the love
of country stepped out on us

thank you for shopping

δ

what is it about this place
that kept her here Rascaline
even as she withered

she made a pact not to sleep in dirt
packed her mouth with tumbleweeds
Victorian Firebox
having lived at half impact
cold social body type contamination

do not doubt every fist
has its perfect eye do not doubt
every eye has its perfect fist

δ

the great head is disturbed

someone was gnawed off my country all
the schoolkids asked was to say tis of usted
your donotcall phone is ringing
call center prisoners wake up to promise
of the number yet to answer

no is not about you
press one if you'd like to be contacted again
to register your opinion in the future

the woman voting off-guard mistaking
laboratory harvest
legislation voicethrowing

the woman off-guard mistaking
body's wellness for wellbeing

the woman offguard mistaking
general population rousted mouth
pact with harrowing facelift canker gullying

when engineering talking to each other
sweat sewn into stitched a gaping
retrieving needlings was asked of us
some tendering of lesion constellatin
lockstep behind each sanction closure

what you will remember are the fools

Morale Boner (30-Second Special)

now delivering to a doorstep near you:
bad omen
divine messenger or
trickster

good deeds come back around
as dogbite

all that racket to talk a drunk down
from the overhang at dirtbike alley
when the fall would be headrush
more than deathwish
but we need a hero here
so the talk talks on
wheelies all around us

the timebomb next door has worn out his narrative welcome
in the shit-you-can't-make-up pantheon of regrets
and slow birds stuffed with what passed as trash
pile up on the curb
in that old chestnut of bird leaving flock
to fight for her dovecote

but gets mixed up with death merchants and swindlers
and becomes a serial nest marauder

not to be romantic
but satellite imagery
makes this place look like somewhere
people would want to live

cigarettes and soda
one each every four hours
four to a room in the nursing home

run out of corners of the house
to move the bedroom away
from bad corners
of course
blue and white didn't mix
then black and white
so it turned out black and blue

how many times does the child have to tell you
dropoffs hoodied down in the car seat are at 6:30 or
he's late for homeroom

but to get back to the dog
same phantom dog loose in your unadjusted eyes
6:30 every morning or he's late and the rest
of the day may as well be insulted away
chasing the dog

we don't do body counts

Morale Boner (Leisure Set)

why is there a ha'penny in Buck's basement?

questions ignite aurora borealis off the plane wing
and we take them along for the ride like the boy band in the leftover
crap rack at Kmart

eloquence surprises in many forms
rancheros and headscarves served up on roller skates
with a piedmont drawl
clear plastic bag sturdy
from emergency room or central booking
either way for once Frankie could see all his stuff in one place
and then something ugly round the corner

your employment
is one big gag order
so less of an insult to be told to shut up
by a cousin or drug dealer

guess we'll lose our jobs
when we crack from working so hard
so we won't lose our jobs

from a football field away
Financing Available
looks like
Fucking Unbelievable

so we wanted to go where the streets
were paved with liquor stores with bars attached
open on Sunday morning
closed for cleaning 6 AM to 10 AM
and we didn't actually have to die and go to heaven

then a few more surprises:
not everyone likes
animals
poetry
or porn
but still on occasion whines about being lonely

a million demonstrators anticipated
couple thousand showed up
disbanded peacefully

at the senior center
nothing stolen

perp entered through an unlatched window
plugged in every electronic device
left unplugged

a blotter such as this should let the honest sleep
except the hole in the window matched
the hole in the heart

what are your neighbors in zip code 21236 watching right now?

Saw
is the thing to see
if seeing *Saw* could be factored into
our GNP the gross
would spank that
of any other nation of ghouls
and per capita we would be
the all-time unstoppable zombie new world power

so you hunkered down and saw *Saw*
and now you have to see *Saw 2*
on the path to *3* seeing *Saw*
bonds your neighbors in your cultural fluency
of football paralysis scene

Indy 500 fireball-fantastic

not to neglect the SWAT team wintering next door

all seen when you thought you'd seen it all

but you had frontyard cutting

alley clearing

dog poop scooping

bullshitting material for weeks

can't hurt to see more *Saw*

Cradle to Grave

Stable

motherfuckers can go from cradle to grave without leaving the block

again the street startles crossing me crossing over

must have GPS'd coordinates for
killing field or rookery

struck as we are on the wrong side at the wrong hour

but people don't wake up every day thinking of somewhere else
mythic surrogate sickly drop into lake water
where you look like a stump
can't see the floor roiling leadshot
cotter pins
backhoe rotor
petrified husk towers
earth mover teeth and blade
auger at the depth
mistaken mother of pearl

no that is the imposition of
another's jarred ancestral complacence
swimming the barbed wire of farm genetics or hustler
what the intellect maw flashed through the still moving pickup
all the while the street still peddling awe

no mistaking bent rims between yards
it's the ground that grounds

dovecote holdover
awning shot through

ledges bunched and overborne
widow's walk seagulled and asea

took time to reconnoiter
swaddling nest anatomy

and account
basketball net
pill bottle cotton
weed eater innards
crapped up dollar bill

trash the street capital

was it peregrine or pigeon

or good vultures in the city of ravens

if sidestepping raptors
glint of exuberance in the gutter
could have triangulated if not for lack of a single point
splintered grid of phantom town square
some have more compass than others

when all you asked for was
leave me my broken body love

Fair

Allrighty
Amos
Antelope
Archer
Banner
Blackie
Black Oak
Blackberry
Blueboy
Booger
Butternut
Carboy
CB
Chili
Chula
Cletus
Confucius
Cotton
Cowboy Troy
Crabshack
Cub
Daddy
Dude
Dundee
Dutch
Echols
Fastpaw
Fatback
Frisoles
Frosty
George Jr.

Granger
Hammer
Hanover
Harpo
Headlight
Hotspur
Joey
Juniper
Kirby
Lemmon
Little Buck
Little Mort
Mascot
Maxwell
Mr. P
Nero
Noser
Oldtime
Opal
Poncho
Pootie
Pops
Poquito
Preacher
Pregonero
Prince
Punch
Quique
Rastus
Rusty
Salt
Samson
Savannah
Shadow

Sheldon
Shep
Shindig
Snicker
Soldier
Stormy
Stryder
T-Bone
Toby J
Tricky
Tubs
Tuxedo
Underdog
Waddles
Yonker
Zane
Zeus

this dog on dog aggression will not stand
cute name but sik puppy in the ring or
roll call of tautologies for
runner or wagerer
president or constituent
goat or satyr
in the dog capital

grocery bags to scoop the carcass
someone slopped with lime

chop shop swap meet

when all the bait is gone and dogs fall out of favor
bring out your cocks
calves

toros
wild ponies

all the while birds buttoned up in her dress
pair of eggs
couplet

Guarded

at closing she walked from Mt Vernon to Bolton Hill barefoot
stripper shoes laced hangdog on her neck
pageant sash welled up in extended blackout

tranced and pixelated body memory for terrain
the lost whatfor as animals

round the time the brewery rehabbed for job creation

and cigarettes still a happy surprise
forever stamp of addictions

glory of opening a book
gilded relief pressed paper
with porcelain sugar doll
for the stolen chapter of benders
sidewinders jags and katzenjammers
yes your lumps paid out in sugar
doll

question was
when the creators of job creation contract creative block

summon the loner tiger kitten
in the outdoor shower
that was a shower in a house
but for the house around it
long folded and dismantled
regenerated into groundswell
compost heap of stray and feral
regrets at the candor

of hugging neighbors
lately bereaved and tending
vinyl wreaths and swags
kicked up in the squall
and now assimilated into
panorama of a passion story
rehab on the scrim

everybody has an Uncle Bill back there somewhere and
the connection turns out roughly the same

though kind to kids and animals

if a partitioned construction site has no peephole

well there's the ax and hammer

somebody had to do the job

curiosity retainer

Critical

zero sum game of the pumproom

sad milling of bad insurance
cattle call
corraling

a boy with unsettling grace
getting to the bottom of snowballs
urge to drink antifreeze
viscous array of days unsorted
sorting out in mechanical mind of the latchkey

children keepers of someone else's rules

as they say the child needs a sorting out
or drunk or klepto or the rat on the fringe
of witness protection

take precosity over languor any day
exchange mean for reckless

what won't be reckoned is the adjuster's code
for cause of the fire when a house
turns incinerator
turns on itself
for turning of
occupant scored a new high
played brokenwing in the yard
last seen in fire chief's hat and cloak
until prodigal

what comes next of course is the getting back
to normal a son on work-release
punches out at Wockenfuss candy
calculates to bandsaw his arm or take
a cherry picker fall
so his mother will reclaim him

what's hard to believe is always overheard

night terror telephone from the halfway house v.
milky foam OD in the driveway
still life with hooker

two different passengers
two different situations
assistance is required

the preacher not
meaning to be preachy said
people who don't believe in anything
don't have children

Serious

less bland affect would be ideal
in the cocktail revolution

cart in the telephone bench
leisure quota
get someone somehow on the horn

piercing wars started and children
devoid of fear of wounding

may have wanted to tuck in with another body
drift through midlife with sex and television
but the parade busts you
you who moved to the hamstrung neighborhood to avoid
Santa atop a firetruck

but long ago traded off sleep for memory

Grave

thing about junkies
they are committed

what the rest of us find exhausting

ferrying kittens from one end of the house to another
on the conjecture there must be a better place
but the mother totes each one back to wean in soot and scavenging
all the while good deed blistering in blindsight
three out of five may live

anything short of lazy
but at some point the junky in you too has to stop moving
bodies at rest as numbers stored in a mobile phone
keep ringing back to the past

this is a call you will want to take

if crackgirl should wander into the yard
during open air fighting
blind poodle in a brownfield
Lonnie says
wind her up
point her home

so says the taxonomist of broken things

wind her up
point her home
ride the rail

ring the attendant
raise your hand now or forever

Jobs

Dreammaker

Dreammaker would appear to live in the Willard lobby
except for the no camping ordinance out the door
local insurgents left battlefield dead to devouring dogs
notwithstanding the people have their dreams
and so Dreammaker has this work to do

not to be self-righteous but the number of clients
dreaming to be Rockettes for a day is
unexpected

and also TV judge

there are infinitesimal digits stitching white thread
into doll's eyes
so they may seem to reflect light

there is the American Typewriter Condensed

scum skimmed from the business trip budget

there is a steady influx of daylight transactions

here in a hotel the word lobbyist was formed and vulgar even then

even now the white glove torquing

sew a drawstring around your life
in an instance you can be gone

hanger sorter

the penalty for overkill in the closed-circuit
speed-dropped size-counts predictive bottom-feeder
failed high school reunion in the oil drum faded town
is

you will wade the carpeted urine light

you will wear security tags in every orifice

your bread will be the dipped snuff of habit

you will monger your neck to the floorplan

and be paid in secondhand last-minutes

needless to say

you are an excellent risk

cigar model

not slow and long but every
morning fucking to work in
New World Theory 7:49 AM
against Historical Bldgs
leading the country in Register
Entries on the way to Avalon
I'd upchucked just beyond
the Versace installation   who are
these people   which Miss America
is most beautiful   in the year 2018
when immortal fathers will be
taken by spaceship   before and
after   read the story and
answer the questions   at
school dances the boys never
asked her to dance then she got
contact lenses   landed in
the second tier of heartthrobs
and policy coattailing erector
set of what has been dismembered
through Rockettes clatter arms
locked with Dream Date Barbie

non-essential services specialist

not to be confused with Dreammaker
the object here to do enough of nothing
but not overperform to ensure
there's always nothing left to do

when a parent says his kid can do that job
this
is the case
when he is correct

but the question arises of whether installing
false bottoms into lipstick cases is non-essential
when the war out there
on runways and reality TV
non-essential furs feathers skins attars
drive inner beauty to the sweatshop
lifetime certificate of non-belonging

just a few more days on the job
and you will have your
non-essential

sent from my fPhone

fabricator automator

work well and no one will work again
but it's a job and not found on the side of the road stuffed inside
some panty hose

a C-note in a toilet will haunt you all your days
I should never have had this but for that hundred
Grandma Hodgie spread it out across a decade
until the trailer burned fatback in the frypan
just as in Charleston the years of bad luck that followed
picking up some strange on the street
and the ugliness you think you came from
not so ugly
when you're buying a smoke for a quarter

then the fabber steps in having encrypted at the polytechnic for the better part of Saturday no time left for drinking and certainly not drinking and tooling down in the hemi to Conowingo to watch for eagles the neighborhood noiseless all the family pets still scrabbling in the yard waste repeat until next Saturday

underwear serger

no women allowed to apprentice in lead type making
lest the babies come out deformed

yet no one better than a woman to walk with the machine

when the rats ate through the paper supply
the single woman amiss in night transit
lives outside schedule for no time glowering in
needing to stay awake for not missing doubling in the night

she would be more frank to slip to present *are*
you talking to me as she is frank in the seduction
of the ruse of talking to me as if there's no hurry
to let the dog out and the dog will never not need
letting out in

the spite for anything treated like a baby

online pharmacy prescription filler

come and get it

we got it
because Buck
had a truck

Day of the Dead sugar skull confectioner

spiced goddamn bullshit
smacked down early morning
as anyone with intimacy of the bloat
of assorted appetites
could call off the dogs

but not the demons

gravecam installer

last reservoir of trust
is tending the dead
reliquary factory
someone's job to get off the phone for a damn second
and put lipstick on it

prop the conscience so the moneybags don't show
a few minutes on this watch and you'll beg for LOL cats

chickenhawks and juveniles fix the mood
in reality TV you thought you paid not to see

the dog you couldn't tell was dead or in a coma all winter
turned out not terminal just incurable

the doves you thought were kicking their chicks
from the cote were the raptor's comeback

who builds a nest on a grave marker
again licked by wilderness

but if we could talk to such a squatter

she may very well say she wouldn't mind playing by the rules

if there were some

Dick Cheney's Heart

the blip in the power grid
is not generators bunkered
or a country song

licked by wilderness
the way licked candy
stripes insinuate into
others' true certified afflictions

the blip in the power grid
is not the key to the city
your grandma never merited for
some cute kid voiceover of
preexisting conditions

the blip is not a grow room
plugged with Quikrete
pain management in the wind

queer way to love your neighbor

the blip is fuckwhatall will fail the body
wagering on a sure thing last bet longshot
or lottery

if there's a line in the sand
it's just beyond the sinoatrial node
first line of defense for the pacemaker

takes less charge to animate a minefield

the grid powers down

the enemy is boredom

flutter murmur afib

and Bone Crusher wins a spot
in the little street heart

prolapse of a better self
buried beneath the brownfields
begotten wilderness

the wizard doesn't live anymore

this calls for extraordinary measures

Dick Cheney's Heart: Revisited

So I picked up Dick Cheney from the hospital and took him to the Fashion Centre at Pentagon City.

He wanted to pick out a Pandora charm for Lynne, the former second lady of the nation.

He pored over the limited edition charms fashioned from children's bones.

I asked, *Dick Cheney, you were once the most powerful oligarch in the universe – what are you doing in a shopping mall?*

He said, *Don't hate on this fine retail establishment. It's an implosive dystopia that props up the master plan.*

Plus, now that he was in semi-retirement, he was thinking about opening a storefront. He has export contacts in Congo.

I said, *Fuck it, Dick Cheney – let's go to Cinnabon.*

He said he couldn't possibly. He needed to start taking better care of his heart.

I said, *Eat your heart out, Dick Cheney.* But I had a conundrum. Should I tell him where his new ticker really came from? Did he lose heart in Kandahar only to find it in Karbala?

Before I could drop that nugget, he made like he had to be somewhere.

He said he'd call a stretch because he thought maybe in his condition he shouldn't be riding in an open truck bed – and also I kinda gave him the creeps.

But what about the second lady's charm?

He said no matter, all along she was a hologram generated in a futile attempt to humanize him. *And no hard feelings*, he told me, *about your decade-plus of personal loathing. It gave me hope in my deepest gravest heart of hearts that I was always doing the right thing. You're a true patriot, Heather Fuller.*

Thanks. Dick.

And then mall security descended and I'm still scrubbing bloody footprints.

Oh, Dick. Once again out of my life.

But in my heart forever.

ALTERNATE ENDING:

Oh, Dick. Once again out of my life.

Tin man motherfucker.

Dick Cheney's Heart: A Memoir

Chapter 1

once again I will wake up and not remember tomorrow

gyspy in the scandal breakfast
you have to stand up to stand down
for all the urban tyrannies that so beguile

more shocking than being sick
is being spared

δ

coincidentally the pit bulldog in the schoolyard
requires all the county's resources

in wargames as in war you wouldn't want
that little buzzsaw catching up with you

all the while the rendition master
perambulates his young adult heart

enough already about Dick Cheney

no one asked to ghostwrite
his sick terrified percussion chamber
so here I am no skirmish forged treaties to encumber

everybody eventually finds the tear
her little life folds back into

if G-Bay had just been one bad blackout
we could mobilize Dick's orange jumpsuit

to flap above the sinkhole

but when it came to blows
his heart hurt

his and mine

δ

transfixed by the fundament
retreating to safehouses

having planned the day around the clock
in the TV show rerun

this is not real time

officer the street is a confusion of secret panels

trumped up as I am I conspired
to be a citizen

stepped on the beer tab with bare feet
tripped over the dog
fell down the stairs
lay on the floor and thought nostalgic thoughts

the order of these events is negotiable

a day in the life [of a ghost]
as they say

Chapter 2

the heart that jumps the track
is a lesson in walking against traffic

the door lady on Belair Road says speed is in this season
for your near-miss little constitutional

shotgun passenger delays gratification
mowing down the dirtbike undertow

no one said recovery was glamorous
and so we idled

δ

pop quiz: who said
I am a very dangerous man.

Charles Manson or Dick Cheney?

in off-the-grid tribunals blood has its day
for the man with no pulse who lives centrifugal
crashing against inner chambers of

puppet hearts
prisons with no boundaries

DNRs for losers

δ

when the pit bulldog turned up

the DNA of a songbird

when a titer derailed an extradition

when Roland Park de-NIMBYed

your broken heart stopped
being a pathology

we learned to hold our liquor

Chapter 3

I woke up on the day of the transplant and

I wanted full disclosure on drones
I wanted cats to stop fucking
I wanted more income disparity at the clinic

I wanted an all-drug option (see Rod Smith, 'Poem')
I wanted to form a girl band with Tina Lynne & Phyllis
I wanted to de-bedazzle

I wanted to put the Fuller in Fullerton
I wanted more sex and less sext
I wanted more aphids

I wanted back-to-back reruns of *Oz*
I wanted to dogear ketamine in the Merck Manual
I wanted everybody to shut up about cicadas

and cherry blossoms
and beavers

I wanted a nonrefundable free pass
I wanted the war on drugs to stop at home [my home] (*ibid.*)
I wanted to like the Krispy Kreme stock ticker

I wanted to feed the badger

I wanted

...

I wanted to see a man about a heart

...

Chapter 4

your broken heart is a syncopated ride with
everyone's favorite reckless driver

which is to say no one's and have something left over
for roadside transgressions

the baby arsonists who light up stray pets and brothers
have more skeletons fossilized into vacant lot dreamtime
than the jury has hangups

which is to say justice must be served
on your own damn time

δ

when I say ethernet I mean literally
there was a net of ether
drifting us to the big sleep undercover

we triaged the meth lab dogs in the open air

someone named the puppies after lipsticks
Ruby
Scarlet
Poppy

I asked my neighbor for his conspiracy
he said it was a long story but
it started with the foreman sliced in half
at Bethlehem Steel

then shutdown
and picket
scabs in the lifeline

docks idling on the union man's clock

δ

the child grounded for roleplaying Omar
lifting jumbo pack of sunflower seeds
Ravens cap
box of Bic lighters

then redistributing along Lanvale

they called him bad for business

I said no
the kid has heart

Chapter 5

why do I have to be such a Dick?

the churchpeople simply wanted a moment
and maybe another prayer lifted up
cannot confuse us further

Michael Vick took his free pass and
read from a script about healing

around the same time the stink bug
became the new cucaracha

my neighbor asked if I could move my stinking motion sensor
so it would stop lighting up her stinking driveway
it was invading her stinking privacy

I took my sweet damn time it's true

δ

the surgeon squares the heart to
the left sternal border

Chris bodyblocked a car to save a kitten
rotator cuff unspiraling

four muscles four tendons four nerves
levitate the arm to praise position

so much can go wrong in the crosshairs
meshes gaps sinuses it's extraordinary
we talk to god at all

my nurse practitioner told me a side effect
could be unusual thoughts

I said well that would be different

so many ways to say sorry
to a friend with birdshot in his heart

Dick Cheney [shooter] is my Stockholm
and my Mardi Gras

but what happened in Kenedy County didn't stay
in Kenedy County

δ

the note on the porch was brief but unequivocal
I think we messed up by putting the birds
back in the nest. Please meet me at the tree.
P.S. Can I hold a 20?

there's no reason why a man with open heart
can't see another day

so many ways to say sorry

I watch birds
livestock for subtlety
signs patterns

bats for cross-pollination
crows for bioburden
error calculus in the food stream

so many ways to say sorry

Chapter 7

my neighbor looked like he had just fallen
from a rock tumbler

the Good Samaritan law allows
touching of strangers and so
the teenager who scored bad black tar
crumpled in my jacket

Foxtrot swept the alley and the spotlight
sliced the bed every 15 minutes

what the hell did someone do
to make us all feel guilty

Uncle Chuck in the piedmont
kept police dispatch rolling in
the front room of the trailer
all day and into the dinner hour

cardiac arrests
drunken and disorderlies
countless bouts of loitering

rogue state of a day
we can't recover

Chapter 8

the preacher said without forgiveness
you eat your heart for breakfast lunch and dinner

in vendetta weather
Sarah Palin became my backup method

off day for sidewalk sales in greater Baltimore
so the game retreated deep into a TV drama

the clerk's defense of the boys who jumped him was
God loves everybody

eat your heart for dinner

δ

the afternoon on Leslie Avenue would be nearly
pastoral but for the veteran looking for his shoes

Bernie told Frankie his sex doll
was bringing down the neighborhood

4 G-Bay hunger strikers cleared for release
gruel rammed down their noses

back in the day Philip Daniel Mitch Randall nearly
slipped away

in roadside trauma stopgap and split second
a punch to the chest
brought the bulldog back

Chapter 9

I had the shift figured out then
the phrase *fecal transplant* crossed my desk

I imagined the Office of the Vice President
felt that way sometimes

Strawberry Blonde put down an opponent
without draining blood

if you wanted a bloodsport
you could have peered into
the dead eye of the blackheart

how colorful it is inside
the human body

δ

my pit bull may not be smarter than your honor student
but she knows when to step away

every day an urban obstacle course

nursing the fading puppies even as
milk failed her

pain jigsawed the morning so we tuned in
heliopad construction racket Platonic
ideal of a medical record

churchpeople came round with ice chips
pocket scriptures

the china was too good to use
so we broke it

Chapter 10

lighting out southward 12-stepped to distraction

no official code for tramps
so we took our cues from snakeheads
catfish fire ants

tents staked outside Prairie Chapel
so many years into a national love affair
with being beaten

the fat lip was a story about
waking up different times every morning
secrets retched from broken face in blackout

Cheney is not Chaney with an 'a'
but for the silent horror

δ

sweet sweat weather and the animals
draw in closer as if called preternatural
to the fire circle

civil disobedient you feel like this sometimes
called in only to burn
or reckon you couldn't help yourself

Chapter 11

the mystery of the day was somebody breaking in
to have a beer and watch some cable

Dominic said it was scandalous
police on bicycles searching for a dog
named Houdini all while
drink was in the wind

music discomfits
the exam room
a patient named Dolores

δ

swamp fever masked road wear
sidewall tear ticking on the open road

febrile retained mystery dose in
the placebo gambit I wanted
to take its vitals with a friend

ride the broad spectrum

toxic shock of allegiance

stammer jive of unnamed ills
in folk we otherwise know

Chapter 12

now the honeycreeper
that is a bird

but her homespun Spanish moss and orchid
boudoir no match
for the preen
of a man who scorched earth

Colonel T. A. Fuller might have meant to say
in *Early Southern Fullers*
the spite of indenture
set brothers against farmstead

sharecropper against slave
revolutionary turned civil
and who recalls what happened to

Ione Fuller
Honor Powell
Cicero Edwards
Parrish Fuller
Zuleike Fuller
Pharisee Powell

some apocrypha of hungry men pressed to sea
to land along the Goshen Swamp
a creekbed sundry

δ

of concern to the G-Bay cleric
detainees licking plaster
blood that wasn't on the breezeway
last time he checked

rehabbed waterfowl fly from captivity
in the shortest route to cover

but no shortcuts in the centering
of a donor heart
splicing nerve and vessel into
a new groove
a stranger rhythm

one terrifying gorgeous mess of
complications

Chapter 13

second crack in the windshield
could give a last damn about
crossfire's path of least resistance and
who's moving into the foreclosure

a dead tree doesn't get any deader after
the 10th person says that tree looks dead
score one for the home owners' association
of your imagination

Mr. Moudry pronounced Reagan like dragon or
raygun depending on his mood and I
got the message

my lifestyle was brackish
my heart:head ratio helter skelter
I had nothing on
the man who dodges bullets

Chapter 14

running out of pretext here
in the bar stool occupation
unsolicited guided detour
to regimentals that wear
the stuck patternmaker's
salvation from the erotic
open air

on different days
poll watcher
interloper
American hero
dictated love of a bygone
trash talk we could get away
with on the coastal plains
but over yonder Montebello
exacted a tenor so surgical
it cut us down

what of bigtops jazz or roadshows
showboat numismatics
nothing says relic like unwinnable war
amnesia of dodged marching orders
heart embalmed in a jar still beating
its cowpie little drum

Chapter 15

to speak of subtext
open rulebook for
sore losers on the ill level field

three Johns on the same block / same side
of the street said the neighborhood
too small for a pit bulldog
while Frankie's stash between 111 and 109
caught no fire

hit by a belt is one thing
a tool belt another
I stopped walking the dog
down Henry
down Alberta
the brindle and I schooled
in intentions of idling cars
stealth meet 'n' greets of
hazardous routines

δ

what happened in absence
was not fondness

heartless not the word I chose
for the repo man
as jobs go
his not chance operation
or algorithm of who receives the placebo
triage priority

deployment orders
bump on the waitlist
air strikes or ground fire

who has a leg to stand on calculating
risk in setting a bone

Chapter 16

so your dog wants club privileges
your hamster a run at Congress

no charge for this diagnosis:
congratulations on your idyllic life

the book Dick didn't write
was a crisis of audience
microtheater of a man hearing himself
when rights were read

every entanglement makes us a little
stupider

try telling Jewel Rita Sharon & Lois
a life loving strangers
was romance for the ages
languishing logjam casualty
on the clinical trial rota

I knew we'd eventually have to close
the bar sleep in the car walk
the backroads home

or go to poetry
to clean the carcass

Chapter 17

we could have aggregated hours
gifted to procedure suites
to resurrect some semblance of a day

disproportionate the body in meting out
its horrors

whatever the prognosis you're still a sinner
and left to drag your sorry sack of trading
cards to other waiting rooms

I'm talking to you Dick Cheney
but especially myself
and any one of you
with a free and happy
hour

δ

if you liked that drone attack you're
going to love North Ave & Gay

a child saw methadone tents and begged
to go to the circus

step right up to glass half full hearts
will go only so tachy before rapid response
snatches back fistful of fibrillation
child in armlock
dog on a chain

Chapter 18

dead rats in pit bull holding
for a minute I forgot Dick Cheney

Lonnie said keep talking like that and
people will think I'm from a town with
even less to recommend it
but discretion is a far roam from the heart

coronary event
you won't mistake it for a party invitation
recall what's left is a grid of falls
picking yourself up til it hurts
losing heart at Step 10

personal inventory:

charley horse
jack leg
funny bone
but mostly a nose for trouble

Lolo's strategy is to sprint the six blocks home
chuck bags and heels if she has to

once inside hit the wall
watch the Clean Street Initiative
from tears in curtains

for a minute I forgot

Chapter 19

Miss Baltimore took a wrong turn
on the way to church sidestepping
blood troughs of upper Broadway
turf besotted hearts *Bon Ami*
scouring down stoops

with rejection risk so high
might as well crown your own damn self
or tick all-of-the-above next time

if war room 2002
had been a multiplayer or
club down Napoleon Alley
we could have thrown down
with our funky moral compass

no wonder
Miss Congeniality
kept a low-grade
buzz on

Chapter 20

old cats know
the one-eyed dog respects the claw
but also naps off-guard

lawless ways of colonial species

Dick Cheney is my Cape Fear
my Graveyard of the Atlantic
cottage in the flood plain

we slept through the Category 4
yard dogs snarling at bogwater creep
rats flushed out from dry dock this
is not allegory but how we held
our cover when things got
weird

myocardium holds charge
as pacemakers power
down powerless heart *ex*
vivo needed a jump from
a Good Samaritan so we rode
it out chased tropical depression
into the eye wall was all
we tendered for love
of country

Chapter 21

country & western
skipping in a filling station
homeland wounds reopen

that refrain of amends

true enough
war is not the answer
it's a bumper sticker
rode hard into a question
bleated heart in mouth

true enough
my one-night stand hat trick is
a roundhouse kick of failure

true enough
lessons of the sick room
flee from me on exit

Little Joe knows the score
American Bull Terrier is still pit bull
unlike truant kids I can't
wheelie through a loophole

Bobby said Dick Cheney had a spirit
on him

there's where I tuned out

that refrain of amends

a heart heals over it beats
the rap

FINIS

EDGE BOOKS

Primitive State *(forthcoming 2015)*	Anselm Berrigan	$15.00
Some Notes on My Programming	Anselm Berrigan	$16.00
Zero Star Hotel	Anselm Berrigan	$16.00
Integrity & Dramatic Life	Anselm Berrigan	$10.00
Once Upon a Neoliberal Rocket Badge	Jules Boykoff	$14.00
The Accordion Repertoire	Franklin Bruno	$16.00
Cipher/Civilain	Leslie Bumstead	$14.00
Crow	Leslie Bumstead and Rod Smith (Eds.)	$8.00
The Golden Age of Paraphernalia	Kevin Davies	$16.00
Comp.	Kevin Davies	$16.00
Shell Game *(forthcoming 2015)*	Jordan Davis	$16.00
American Whatever	Tim Davis	$12.00
The Julia Set	Jean Donnelly	$6.00
Tachycardia *(forthcoming 2015)*	Buck Downs	$16.00
Ladies Love Outlaws	Buck Downs	$5.00
Marijuana Softdrink	Buck Downs	$11.00
clearing without reversal	Cathy Eisenhower	$14.00
World Prefix	Harrison Fisher	$6.00
Metropolis XXX: The Decline and Fall of the Roman Empire	Rob Fitterman	$14.00
Metropolis 16–20	Rob Fitterman	$5.00
One Hundred Etudes	Benjamin Friedlander	$16.00
Dovecote	Heather Fuller	$14.00
perhaps this is a rescue fantasy	Heather Fuller	$14.00
Flarf Orchestra *(audio CD)*	Drew Gardner	$12.99
Terminal Humming	K. Lorraine Graham	$15.00
Non/Fiction	Dan Gutstein	$14.00
Sight	Lyn Hejinian and Leslie Scalapino	$15.00
Late July	Gretchen Johnsen	$4.00
Mannerism	Deirdre Kovac	$18.00
Deer Head Nation *(forthcoming 2015)*	K. Silem Mohammad	$16.00
Monsters *(forthcoming 2015)*	K. Silem Mohammad	$16.00
Breathalyzer	K. Silem Mohammad	$15.00
The Sense Record and Other Poems	Jennifer Moxley	$14.00
Heteronomy	Chris Nealon	$16.00
Plummet	Chris Nealon	$15.00

I GOOGLE MYSELF *(forthcoming 2015)*	Mel Nichols	$16.00
CATALYTIC EXTERIORIZATION PHENOMENON	Mel Nichols	$16.00
STEPPING RAZOR	A.L. Nielsen	$9.00
STRUCTURE FROM MOTION *(forthcoming 2015)*	Tom Raworth	$15.00
CALLER AND OTHER PIECES	Tom Raworth	$12.50
ACE	Tom Raworth	$12.00
DOGS	Phyllis Rosenzweig	$5.00
INTERVAL	Kaia Sand	$14.00
YOUR COUNTRY IS GREAT: HAITI–NICARAGUA *(forthcoming 2015)*	Ara Shirinyan	$18.00
CUSPS	Chris Stroffolino	$4.00
LONG TERM RAISIN *(forthcoming 2015)*	Ryan Walker	$16.00
FELONIES OF ILLUSION	Mark Wallace	$15.00
HAZE: ESSAYS, POEMS, PROSE	Mark Wallace	$14.00
NOTHING HAPPENED AND BESIDES I WASN'T THERE	Mark Wallace	$9.50
THIS CAN'T BE LIFE	Dana Ward	$16.00

AERIAL MAGAZINE

(EDITED BY ROD SMITH)

Aerial 10: LYN HEJINIAN, *co-edited by Jen Hofer (forthcoming 2015)*	$25.00
Aerial 9: BRUCE ANDREWS	$15.00
Aerial 8: BARRETT WATTEN	$16.00
Aerial 6/7: FEATURING JOHN CAGE	$25.00

Literature published by Aerial/Edge is available through Small Press Distribution (www.spdbooks.org; 1-800-869-7553; orders@spdbooks.org) or from the publisher at P.O. Box 25642, Georgetown Station, Washington, D.C. 20027. When ordering from Aerial/Edge directly, add $2.00 postage for individual titles. Two or more titles postpaid. For more information, please visit our Web site at www.aerialedge.com.